I0098044

"15 Questions Teens Would Like To Ask Their Parents- But Don't"

Lawrence R. Mathews

www.inspirationalphilosophy.com
lrmathews60@yahoo.com
480-495-3309

Published by Lawrence R. Mathews Opening
The Way

Library of Congress Control Number:
2012923997

The author is available for lectures and may
be reached at the phone number and/or e-
mail address above.

Book Cover Design: Coni Bourin
Editing: Bill Drummonds

ISBN: 0-9786346-5-9

"Do Not Allow What You Think or How You Think to LIMIT What You Think or How You Think!"

-Lawrence R. Mathews

Table of Contents

Dedication

This book is dedicated to every student I had the privilege of instructing during my time as a teacher at schools within the Glendale Elementary School District during the 2007-2011 school years. This experience taught me that contrary to what some say, the future of our nation is bright. At least as long as we adults "listen" to what the youth are asking of us. They do want our guidance as they learn how to grow into responsible adults. As long as we live the types of lives we want them to emulate, our nation will be fine. However, if we don't, then the future is uncertain at best.

There are a few specific young people that I want to acknowledge. They reviewed the answers provided to the questions enclosed and advised me on what needed to be done to make them understandable for youth readers. I am proud to say that at the time of their reviews, all of them maintained at minimum a 3.0 grade point average.

Shelby Drushel;
Elizabeth C. Ferrendelli;
Garrett P. Freiwald;
Jesus Gonzalez Jr;
Jennifer Gutierrez;
Matthew Lund;
Claire Marasigan;
Nailah Mathews;
Van Nguyen;
Missy O'Neil;
Nargish Patwoary;
Karim Ramierz-Soto and;
*Elizabeth Rodriguez Guerra who first suggested that my advice to youth would make a good book project.

Youth Introduction

This is an interesting time in your life isn't it? Some days you feel like an adult. Other days you feel like a kid who can't make up your mind about the simplest of things. On top of that you are being pressured from many areas about a variety of things.

There is pressure to fit in which shows up differently for different people. For some teenagers fitting in means not doing well in school while for others it means excelling in it. Fitting in can also mean doing things you're not comfortable with such as using drugs, drinking alcohol and having sex before you are ready.

Then there is the pressure you get from your parents who want you to be a certain way. They want you to act a certain way. They also want you to think a certain way.

So you are faced with your friends, who want you to be one way, and your parents who want you to be another. You are in the middle being pulled both ways. You shouldn't be surprised to find this experience a difficult one to handle. A tug-of-war game is being played and you are the rope!

The reality is that you are currently in the process of discovering who you are. What ways are you like your parents? What ways are you like your friends? What ways are you different from each? Your body is also changing from a child's body to an adult one. These hormonal changes also create their own pressures and challenges as you grow up a little bit more each day. This is why your moods can change so quickly.

One thing that parents don't always do well is listen to you. There are many things you have questions about which requires advice. However, because we sometimes still see you as our small child of 5 or 6 instead of the teenager you are, often we don't hear you. So the times you would like or need to talk to us you don't because we allow ourselves to believe we already know what you are thinking and need.

For you, our inability to listen gives you a reason to stop communicating what you need from us. This is unfortunate, because often you teenagers don't always know what it is that you need or want from us. You just know that something is happening and you need assistance. You would like help but don't know what to ask for. This makes your communication with us difficult when you are ready to actually talk. However, you quickly stop these efforts when you realize that we think we already know everything before we allow you to say what's on your mind.

We should not be surprised when you then seek guidance and assistance from your friends. Although they lack the experience to give you good advice, they at least know what it is that you need since they may be feeling the same way.

This book contains **15 Questions** about parents that you as my students over the past four years told me you would like to ask your parents - but don't. Other questions that you would like to ask us on a variety of other subjects will be released in a more comprehensive book sometime next year.

Some of the answers I am sure you will like. Others I am sure you will not like. However, all of them will help you more easily deal with some of the issues that are common with young people your age.

Parental Introduction

Raising teenagers can be an interesting endeavor. As an educator of junior high school students for 12 years, and as the father of an adult and 15 year-old-teenager, I speak from experience. Although raising children through the teenage years has many fulfilling moments, there are many times when all we can do is scratch our heads and wonder, "What was I thinking when I decided to become a parent?"

Have you ever asked your teenager a question that you thought was simple and they looked at you as if you had asked them an algebraic equation? How many of you routinely receive the following answers no matter the question posed?

a) Fine;
b) Good;
c) Okay;
d) I don't know.

Does it ever matter what question is being asked? One of the four answers above is usually one of the answers that you get from teenagers. This you know from the experiences you have with your own children. As an educator, this is what I have seen in large school settings also.

I think it is safe to say that one of the challenges in raising teenagers is that we as parents have a difficult time communicating with them. This combined with their difficulty communicating with us has led to the present parent-teenager dynamic. This is why they provide us with these short types of answers.

Difficulty communicating is not always a bad thing when those times are intermittent and short-lived. However, the inability to know what's going on in our teenagers' lives during these important adolescent years over a prolonged time period can negatively impact their maturation process from teenager to adult.

The "**15 Questions Teens Would Like To Ask Their Parents - But Don't,**" book is a compilation of questions that teenagers have asked me over the last four years I taught in the public school setting. This was during some of those rare moments when I was able to get an actual answer out of them lol!. They are questions that they said they would like to ask their parents or parental figures but generally don't because of the response they might get from them. In fact, these questions are one section from a more comprehensive book I am currently writing. It will provide other questions from a cross-section of topics that they would also like answers to. Additional questions they don't feel comfortable asking. It was the students who suggested that I turn these questions into a book for them based upon the advice I provided to them while teaching.

But these questions are just as important for you Mom and Dad as they provide you with a clear idea of what your children are thinking. Therefore these questions can be used to foster a discussion that can lead to more open lines of communication between you and your teenager.

Did You Know?

*Depression Statistics in Teenagers

1. Teen depression is so common that almost 10-15% of teenagers experience some kind of depressive symptoms during their teen days.
2. Around 5% of teenagers have been diagnosed with major depression at some point of time.
3. Teens suffering from depression for at least a year have been the condition for 8.3%.
4. The prevalence of teenage depression is more for teenage girls compared to boys. The risk factor is also high for the teenagers with previous depression attack, long term disability, trauma, abuse or family history.

   *CDC/NCHS National Health and Nutrition Examination Survey 2005-2006

Question One:

Why do I feel more comfortable telling my friends personal secrets than I do my parents?

Answer:

Because you probably believe that your friends can relate better to your personal secrets than your parents can. Your friends are the same age as you. They may have had the same situation happen to them. They may have even had their own parents react to the situation the same way that your parents have reacted. So as you stated in the question, it's just more comfortable.

A big part of it though is that the secret is possibly something that you may not be proud of. Something you don't want your parents to know about because they would be disappointed in you. In fact you may be ashamed of what you did, if it happened in the past; or something you're thinking about doing in the future. Although it does not always seem to be the case, I have found that young people really don't want to let their parents down or disappoint them.

Of course the last reason is the most obvious one: you don't want to get into trouble.

17

Be careful though. Depending upon the personal secret, telling your friends instead of your parents might not really help you. Especially if it is something that only an adult can help you with, such as physical or sexual abuse.

So this is pretty much it. You are more comfortable telling your friends your personal secrets because you relate better to them and you probably believe that you will get into trouble if you tell your parents.

Did You Know?

•American teenagers spend 31 hours per week watching television.

•17 hours a week listening to music.

•3 hours a week watching movies.

•4 hours a week reading a magazine.

•10 hours a week online.

•That's 10 hours and 45 minutes a day of video consumption.

Question Two:

Why don't parents listen to their kids?

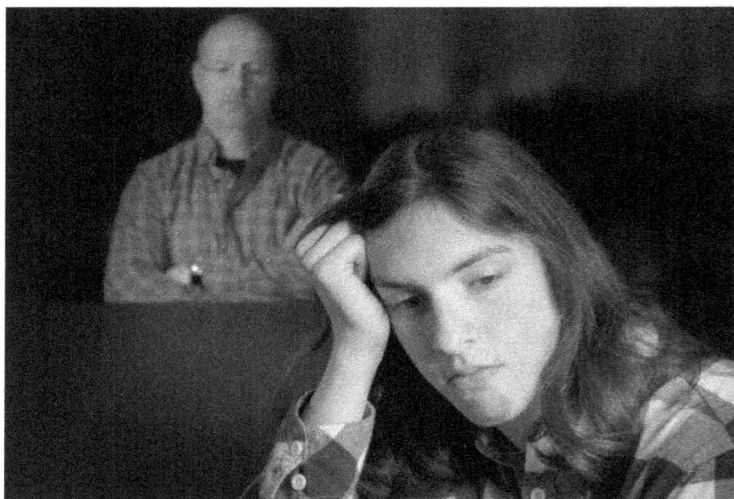

Answer:

Parents don't listen to their kids for a few reasons. First, how much can a child tell a parent, realistically speaking?

-A lesson in school that the parent has never received? Probably.

- A news event that the parent has not heard about? Sure.

-A recipe that a parent has never seen before? Definitely.

But life experience issues are another story. Experience cannot be minimized. Your parents and other adults have lived a long time. They are still alive, which means they have learned how to survive. This is not an easy thing to do. Although people take it for granted, many people died because they were at the wrong place at the wrong time. Some died because they engaged in an activity that wasn't good for them. Others ate the wrong types of foods, or because they smoked or drank or used drugs, died earlier than they should have. And still others committed suicide because they found life to be too difficult.

Contrary to the way it is depicted on television, life is VERY hard. It is not easy. An ancient African Kamitic proverb describes it like this:

"Grief is natural to the mortal world and is always about you; pleasure is a guest and visiteth by thy invitation. Use well thy mind and sorrow shall be passed behind you. Be prudent and the visits of joy shall remain long with you."

Parents don't listen to their teenager's because they know this about life and teenager's don't. Parents don't want their teenager's lives being any harder than they have to be. This is why parents don't listen to their teenager's. Simply stated, kids just don't understand☺.

Did You Know?

Possible Effects of Stress in Children and Teens

•30% of "tweens," children between the ages 8-12, and 42% of teens say they get headaches at least once a week with only 13% of parents reporting to being aware of their children having headaches.

•39% of tweens and 49% of teens report difficulty sleeping with only 13% of parents reporting their awareness of children sleep problems.

•25% of tweens and 39% of teens reported eating too much or too little due to stress. Only 8% of parents reported being aware of this behavior.

Question Three:

Why is it that parents can get mad and then act like a child and ignore you, but if we teenagers do the same thing we get into even more trouble?

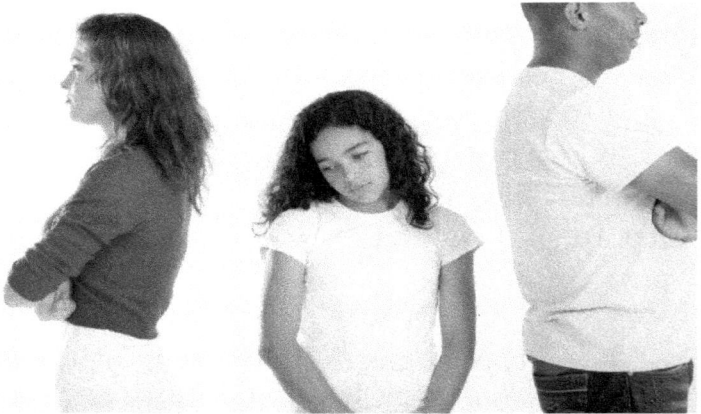

Answer

This is an example of parents being engaged in the practice of "Do as I say and not as I do!" Remember that your parents are not perfect! We have our own moments where we also make mistakes. Often, in our desire to do what's right for you, we do things for reasons that are not always clear. Sometimes we get too emotional. When this happens it is easy for us to stop being the adult and instead react in ways that could be considered childish. Ignoring someone because they are mad could be considered childish. So when we begin ignoring you because we are upset, leave us alone until we calm down. The situation will be worse if you keep talking. Continue the conversation when we calm down and we can speak more rationally.

As for you teenagers not being able to do the same thing, recognize that if you ignore us while we are talking to you, we consider this to be disrespectful. As your parents we believe that you have an obligation to listen and not ignore what we say. You will get in more trouble when you ignore your parents because parents do not want to be disrespected.

So this is indeed a case of parents being able to do something, ignore you when they are upset, that you are not allowed to do when you feel the same way. While I do believe that this is unfair, right now at least, it's just the way it is.

Did You Know?

<u>Stress Among Teenagers</u>

According to the American Psychological Association, 2009 survey, stress among teens and their parents is rising significantly every year. Stress in children is being reported more often by school counselors, social workers and psychologists. Adolescent psychologists report that many parents who are seeking professional help have to wait (as long as three months) to get their child an appointment to meet with someone to help their child or teen reduce their stress.

Question Four:

I don't understand my parents at all.

Answer:

That shouldn't be surprising. It is difficult to understand anything that you haven't experienced for yourself. Have you ever had a friend do something strange and you could not figure out why they did it? Even when they told you, did you understand why they did it?

It's difficult for anyone to understand why someone else thinks the way they do and acts the way they do for one simple reason: we don't think or act the way they do. That's the only way to truly understand something, to be in the same position with the same choices with the same set of life circumstances and experiences. An old saying says "You must walk in my shoes, to know where I've been." This goes for parents as well.

One thing you can do though is understand general tendencies about people. You can develop an awareness that people in the same place at the same time in the same circumstance will generally tend to respond in the same way. That's why many different parents respond the same way to raising their kids. This is also why many kids become the same types of parents when they get older.

Not understanding your parents should not surprise you. For the rest of your life don't be surprised to find that there will be far more things you will not understand about them than things you do. But do not give up hope. Your day will come! One day you will understand your parents. That day will come when you become a parent yourself! ☺

Did You Know?

Stress can come in many forms for children and teens. School, activities, friends and family are often reported as the "stressor points" for children today. To begin to understand the scope of the problem, here are some basic stats for teenage stress in the U.S. today:

•45% of teens (ages 13-17) said that they were more worried in 2009 when only 28% of their parents reported teen and child stress increased.

•30% of children reported stress about the family's financial or economic situation when only 18% of parents reported that finances were a cause of their children's stress.

Question Five:

I love my mom but can't talk to her. I'm older now and I'm having issues with my dad. Is this normal and how can I change it for the better?

Answer:

First, as it relates to your mom, it is quite normal for young people 12-16 to have difficulty talking to their parents. There are many reasons for this. Many parents find it very difficult to communicate with their children because they have a difficult time letting their children grow up. Sometimes parents don't know how to let go.

Another reason is that parents often believe that if their children are asking about something that means that they must be ready to do something. For example, if you ask your parents about sex, rest assured they will be thinking that you must want to try it.

And finally I think it is fair to say that in general parents never learned how to communicate with their children because their parents never communicated with them. Parents often raise their children the way they were raised. Unfortunately this is not always great. These are a few of the reasons parents have difficulty communicating with their children.

To change this communication gap with your mother for the better, keep in mind what I said above about the three reasons we have difficulty communicating with you. Then tell your mom you have something you want to talk to her about. Let her know you want her advice and information only and that nothing has happened for her to get upset about. (Unless something has happened that she has a reason to get upset about☺). Tell her what you have to say. Then do not expect her to react. She may either get quiet or tell you she needs to think about what you said, or she may start talking immediately. Whatever she does, realize that at this point she is processing what you said. Don't take everything she says immediately seriously, because at this point she is just thinking about what you said. A lot of people need to talk while they are thinking. So if she starts immediately talking, this is probably what she is doing. Either way, after you have said your piece and she has said a bit of hers, ask her if you both can finish the conversation later on that day or the next. She will need this time to reflect not only on what you said, but also on your level of maturity in approaching her this way. I guarantee when you complete the conversation, the two of you will actually be able to talk. This does not mean that she will agree with what it is you might be requesting, but it does mean that the door of communication between the both of you will be open for days and years to come.

The issues with your dad present a different type of situation. If the issues involve strictly communication type issues, then these can be handled the same way that I mentioned above with your mother. As men, we may get a bit more hyper, but some of us can be a bit calmer when our children begin acting like young adults. If you handle the conversation like this, maturity is what you will be showing. But if the issues with your Dad involve conduct by him which is inappropriate and cause you to feel uncomfortable in any way (physical, emotional, or sexual abuse), then the authorities should be contacted immediately if you do not feel comfortable sharing this with your mother.

Question Six:

What should I do so that my parents will trust me?

Answer:

Since you're asking this question does this mean that you have given your parents a reason not to trust you? ☺ Has something happened that has given your parents a reason to think that you are untrustworthy? Do your parents have a reason to not believe what you say?

Consider that there are two types of people who are typically not trusted. Those who "speak with forked tongues," or lie, as the Native Americans used to say, and those who do not do the things they say they are going to do. These two types of people are not reliable and are considered to be untrustworthy. Think about it: have you dealt with a person who promised to do something for you but they always let you down? How long did it take before you stopped trusting them?

So the best way to gain the trust of parents, and people in general, is to not be either of these types of people. Trust, like many things in life, is something that has to be earned. It is not something that a person can get overnight. With your parents this can be done or re-established by developing the two following habits.

First, speak truthfully at all times. Second, do what you say you will do all the time without fail!

As it relates to speaking truthfully at all times consider that once your parents not only believe you are telling them the truth, they will soon have no reason to doubt the truth of anything you have to say. Soon they will start to know that what you say is true. At this point trust will easily be gained. Why? Because they will no longer have a reason to wonder what you are up to.

I know this is something you may not even believe is possible. Speaking truthfully at all times in this society is not an easy thing to do. Unfortunately it is common to see people regularly speak untruthfully. People lie when they have done something they should not have done. They also lie about small, inconsequential things. Why? Some people are cowards and don't want to face the consequences of their actions. Others lie for no reason at all. But this is how you gain trust. By being a leader and not doing what everyone else does, which means developing the internal strength to face the consequences and accept responsibility for your own actions.

The second way to gain trust is by doing what you say you are going to do at all times without fail. This means that you become a reliable person, someone upon whom others can depend.

Now there will be times when circumstances will prevent you from doing something you may have promised. This is okay as long as you let those who were depending on you know about the change and what the change will be before the act was supposed to be done. Always allow the other person to have time to make different plans or arrangements.

If you do these two things consistently, it will lead to the type of trust that you say you want from your parents and everyone else as well.

Question Seven:

Should you tell your parents if you smoke?

Answer:

Why not tell your parents? Are you ashamed of what you are doing? If what you are doing is so wonderful, why not share it with those who love you more than anyone else? The only reason a person would want to hide this from their parents is if they were actually ashamed of what they were doing right? ☺

There are many reasons to feel ashamed of this conduct. Smoking leads to different types of cancers. The latest statistics indicate that one out of every two people in the USA who die do so because of some type of cancer. Smoking also increases the amount of adrenaline in your blood stream. Essentially this makes your heart beat faster. This is not a good thing because it leads to high blood pressure which makes it easier for a person to get heart disease. Heart disease is a leading cause of death.

Other than how cool smoking seems to be, what's positive about it? So, telling your parents about a smoking habit should not be that big of a deal if you are comfortable that there is no harm in what you are doing.

Did You Know?

TEENAGER DEPRESSION

CDC/NCHS National Health and Nutrition Examination Survey 2005-2006

Depression is a common problem all over the world, not only for the adults but also for teenagers. As per the latest Statistics, almost 5.3% of the adult US population is diagnosed for some kind of mental disorder every year, which comes to be approximately 17 million people. **In case of teenagers, about 20% of total population gets diagnosed with serious depressed condition before they reach their adulthood.**

Question Eight:

Can you truly rely on your parents? Do they really know what's best for us?

Answer:

If you are between the ages of 12-16 and have lived with your parents all or most of that time it is safe to say that you can rely on your parents. They have raised you and provided the means for you to be where you are today. You don't live on the streets. You probably eat regularly. You have clothes to wear. Although you may want a lot more than just these things, the fact of the matter is that you have them. These are called basic necessities or basic needs. That's more than can be said of people in other parts of the world and some parts of the USA. So it's safe to say that you can rely on your parents to take care of your basic needs.

Whether parents really know what's best for you can be looked at in a couple of ways. First, you must keep in mind that your parents at one time were also teenagers. So the experiences you are having today they have already experienced, and probably more than once. So some of the advice they give is based upon what they have been through and personally experienced.

Second, those that did not personally experience what you may be going through know a great deal about the characteristics of people. Because parents are older, they have gotten used to the different personality types of people in general. That's why they may look at one of your friends and tell you that they are "trouble" before they get to know them because they have known "trouble" types before.

Finally, your parents, like all adults, have made mistakes in their younger days from which they have learned. Parents want to protect their children from making the same mistakes so they attempt to keep their children from experiencing the same type of painful lessons they had when they were younger.

Do parents know what's best for their kids? Who knows what's best for anyone or anything? All anyone can do is the best they know how to do at any given time. Certainly, parents care about you far more than anyone on the street does. This might not seem to be the case depending upon how your parents act emotionally. But deep down inside they do care about you a great deal. Parents want the best for you. Is there anything better than that?

Question Nine:

What can a kid do when a parent takes their anger out on them?

Answer:

A lot of it depends on whether the anger is expressed physically as in abuse or mentally in the form of yelling. If the anger comes out through physical abuse then you have to protect yourself. This might mean leaving the room, or calling someone like your other parent, a relative, friend or even the police. Unfortunately for those young people who experience this type of behavior from their parents, this type of conduct is not new. Therefore, there will be signs that the angry parent is about to become angry. It could be when they start drinking, or when they're paying the bills. An angry parent will have a pattern to their anger, so getting to know the pattern will allow you to remove yourself from the situation before the anger comes and is taken out on you.

Mentally, you must be careful not to attach a meaning to the angry parent's behavior. Some young people mistakenly allow themselves to believe that they (the teenager), have done something wrong. This is called "internalizing the conduct." This is the worst thing that can be done because teenagers may blame themselves for the action instead of the angry parent.

DON'T DO THIS! Severe emotional harm can occur if you blame yourself for a parent's actions.

Also don't feel sorry for the angry parent. No matter what happened that triggered anger in this parent, taking this out on a young person is inexcusable. Negative things happen to everyone. Wishing that circumstances would improve is okay. However, feeling sorry for an adult who is wrongfully taking their anger out on a child is not helpful to them or you.

Finally, recognize that the way the angry parent is handling the situation is not the best or only way to handle it. Resolve within yourself that when the type of circumstance that makes a parent angry develops in your own life you will handle it differently. You will handle it with patience and poise. Make sure you do this, because it is common for people who have been mistreated with anger to also treat others in an angry way. You don't want to start treating others the way you may have been treated. A great practice is to actually do unto others as you would have them do unto you!

Question Ten:

How do I deal with my parents' constant fighting?

Answer:

Before I go too deeply into this answer, let's be clear that we're talking about the same thing. Your question appears to be asking about parents who "physically" fight with each other. An answer for this question is much different than an answer that refers to parents who argue a lot. Some teenagers think arguing is fighting. My in-depth answer below will address the parents who fight physically. However, for those who think arguing is fighting, be aware that you may be wishing for something only seen in the movies. People together, especially in a committed relationship like your parents, are not always going to agree on things. This is a fact of life that you will need to get used to. Although it would be great if they had a calmer way of making joint decisions, apparently this is how they interact with each other. So short, of them physically fighting with each other, arguing is a part of being in relationships. Everyone will argue and disagree about something. If this is the case, consider talking to them about how their arguing makes you feel during a time they are calm. They will appreciate it and I'm sure that they will work to not argue around you as much. However, if they don't do this, it's not personal. They may not know how to communicate in any other way but this.

Now for those of you with parents who fight physically, keep the following three things in mind. First, don't think that you can get them to stop. Although it would not hurt to speak with each one of them privately when they are not fighting, and tell them how you feel when they do; don't expect them to stop. They have probably been fighting for a long time and are used to it now. Sitting them down during the calm moments and sharing with them how their fighting makes you and maybe your siblings feel may help. If you do this they will respect your maturity and will remember this the next time they get upset with each other. Under no circumstances though should this be done when they are fighting! This will make the situation worse. At that point, depending on how the bad the fighting is, it's probably best to call another relative or maybe even the police.

Second, recognize that the fighting has nothing to do with you. A lot of times teenagers believe that it is their fault that their parents fight. It's not, so don't allow yourself to believe this. Also, don't fool yourself into believing they should stop fighting because you want them to. Deep down they probably don't want to fight with each other. However, they have probably gotten so used to dealing with each other in this way that they have not yet learned how to stop it. So don't make their fighting become an issue about you.

Third, do not ever allow yourself to believe that fighting is okay for couples. Many young people who grew up with parents who fought wind up fighting with their mate when they become adults. This is one of the reasons that they say "the fruit doesn't fall too far from the tree." Never accept that fighting is okay. Always vow that you will never do this in your relationships. Finally, when you fully mature, desire only to be with people who don't want to fix problems by fighting with you.

Question Eleven:

How come teenagers don't really take in what their parents tell them?

Answer:

People only take in information that they believe will help them. Generally, people only listen to those people that they think know more than they do. Why would anyone listen to someone they believe knows less than them? For a variety of reasons teenagers tend to think that they know more than their parents. This is strange given that teenagers are much younger than their parents and are experiencing for the first time what their parents have probably experienced many times before.

I have been told by other teenagers that they don't believe what their parents say because they believe that life for them is different today than it was when their parents were teenagers. There may be some validity in this belief. However, your parents still know more about life in general than you do because they have lived longer than you.

Many adults felt the same way when they were teenagers. Many of us were unable to realize that our parents had ever been young people. They had always been nothing but

57

"old" parents. Nothing more and nothing less. So not thinking that they can relate to you is quite normal. However, teenagers would be wise to listen to their parents for two reasons: one, because they actually do love and want the best for you; and two; because they actually do know more about things than you do.

Did You Know?

In the last 45 years **suicide rates have increased by 60% worldwide**. Suicide is among the three leading causes of death among those aged 15-44 years in some countries, and the second leading cause of death in the 10-24 years age group; these figures do not include suicide attempts which are up to 20 times more frequent than completed suicide."

Source:
http://www.who.int/mental_health/preventio n/suicide/suicideprevent/en/

Question Twelve:

How do I handle the fact that my dad is in jail?

Answer:

Consider the following four things. First, do not allow yourself to think that being in jail is okay. There are more than a few people who think that it is okay to get in trouble and go to jail because they have family members there. That is not the case. Jail is a place where you and your freedoms are taken away. Additionally, you get a record which makes it almost impossible to get a job when you get out. So do not let yourself believe that being in jail is okay. It is not because it makes the lives of you and your family very difficult.

Second, do not feel sorry for yourself. Although you may have to do more around the house that's okay because no one can control what their life situation will be. What you can do is control how you respond to it. So if you have to help out more, so be it. This will make you stronger if you accept the challenge instead of feeling sorry for yourself.

Third, do not make your dad wrong for being in jail. Although he may have done something stupid or wrong to be placed there, your being mad or angry at him will hurt you far worse than it will hurt him. Being angry or upset like this can build up inside of you as stress, and over time can lead to anxiety which can lead to physical problems. It can also make you an angry person who takes things out on other people. You have seen these types of people before: people who blow up and get mad at others very quickly for what seems like very little reasons? There is a reason they just don't realize what it is. The reason is that the frustration, pain, and hurt that is kept inside eventually builds up too much and at some point has to come out. Just like volcanoes erupt when there is a lot of pressure inside of them, people explode emotionally when there is a lot of pressure inside of them. This is not a good thing because if this happens to you the result from your explosion may put you in the same place in which your dad has found himself.

And finally, take the experience and use it as a motivation to succeed in life. Look at the impact your dad's being in jail has made on you and the rest of your family. Then vow to make sure that you will do whatever it takes to make sure that you never allow yourself to be placed in that same circumstance.

If you use any one of these four, you will be fine. If you use all four, you will effectively turn the negative situation of your dad's being in jail into a positive motivational movement for you.

Question Thirteen:

Why do some parents find it difficult telling their kids that they love them?

Answer:

Be aware that a person's inability to express their love for someone else does not mean that they do not love them. What it simply shows is that they have trouble saying it. That's all it means and this is important to know. So don't think that your parents do not love you if they don't tell you this. In actuality this is not the case and most often not true.

First, consider that parents, like other people, (especially men); do not typically express their emotions. In fact, a case can be made that men in this society are taught that it is not manly to show their emotions. It is common to hear someone say "be a man" and "suck it up" when a male might be close to showing some type of emotion. Males who grow up thinking like this will become men who will act like this. They will find it difficult to tell their children they love them. They will also find it difficult to tell their wives or other members of their family that they love them also. So this is one of the reasons parents find it difficult.

It is also common for parents to raise their children the same way they were raised. So a parent who grew up never having their own parents tell them that they loved them will treat their children-you-the same way they were treated when they were kids. It's like the phrase which says, "You can't give what you never had!"

Finally, the definition of what you consider love to be might be different from your parents'. For example, some people think that actions are a manifestation of love. Providing for one's family, shelter, food, and clothing is considered by some to be the signs that they love them. You may have heard them say, "Why would I have done all these things for you if I did not love you?" If you believe that love is shown when someone actually tells you this, then you will probably have a mistaken view of what this parent is thinking.

It is more likely than not that a parent who does not tell their child that they love them is a person who expresses their love differently than the way you may want or feel like you need. This parent is probably the type

66

who expresses their love through their actions. This parent probably will not say it. I think it's safe to say, then, that it's probably not a case of your parents not loving you; more likely it's a case of you not realizing how they show it.

Question Fourteen:

How do I deal with my Dad being drunk all the time?

Answer:

Very carefully!

A lot of this depends on how your Dad acts when he is drunk. Some people fall asleep, others get loud. Still others get physical and start fights with others. Whichever way he acts, a drunk in the house is difficult to deal with for everyone.

No matter which type of drunk he is, staying out of his way is the best thing to do. Sleeping drunks need to be left alone so nature can take its course while they sleep it off. Loud drunks like to argue. Of course, since they are drunk what they say makes no sense so it's pointless talking to them. Plus, loud drunks tend to knock things over since they are drunk and then blame it on those who happen to be around. Fighting drunks can be dangerous because they are unpredictable and those around them can get hurt. Staying away from this type of drunken person until they are sober is the best thing you can do.

One thing to be mindful of is the feelings you may get when your dad is drunk. It is common to feel bad when you see a loved one like this in this condition. Do your best not to make his conduct personal to you. His drunkenness is not your fault nor is it a reason to believe that being drunk around the family is okay. This is your dad's issue and his only. Use this to remind yourself of how you will not be when you grow older and mature into an adult.

Did You Know?

<u>Underage Drinking</u>

More than 10 million youths, ages 12 to 20, in this country report they have consumed alcohol in the past 30 days. The rate of current alcohol consumption increases with increasing age according to the 2010 National Survey on Drug Use and Health from 2% at age 12 to 21% at age 16, and 56% at age 20.

Question Fifteen:

How can I understand my parents more?

Answer:

This is a very mature question. Understanding your parents more is not difficult. All you have to do is place yourself in their shoes every time they do something that you don't agree with or understand. For example, if you want to stay up late and they say no, consider what you would do if you had a child your age asking the same thing. What would your answer be to your child?

Also, when placing yourself in their shoes, consider that when your parents were younger they may have gotten into trouble by doing what you are asking them to let you do right now. Make sure you factor this into the decision making process when you listen to their answer.

The short answer to the question is that your parents want the best for you. They don't want you to make the same mistakes they did. They want your lives to be easier than theirs were. The decisions they make about you are typically done with your best interests in mind. They want to help and protect you. This is what they are always attempting to do. Once you fully realize this, understanding your parents becomes quite easy! ☺

Glossary of Questions

How come teenagers don't really take in what their parents tell them?

How do I handle the fact that my Dad is in jail?

Why do some parents find it difficult telling their kids that they love them?

How do I deal with my dad being drunk all the time?

How can I understand my parents more?

Note About the Author

Lawrence R. Mathews helps people to live life well!

Lawrence R. Mathews, J.D., B.B.A., draws on his professional and personal experiences to allow others to view life as full of opportunities. He translates complex philosophies into practical steps for creating a life full of joy and abundance.

His diverse background includes a Bachelor's degree in Business Administration and teaching in both the Detroit, Michigan and Glendale, Arizona school systems. The first in his immediate family to graduate from college, he then earned his law degree practicing as a trial attorney. As an attorney he has practiced before the Michigan Supreme Court.

He is a businessman, motivational speaker, author of several articles and the following books:

1. "There Must Be A Better Way of Doing This!"

2. "You Are Responsible For Your Life!"

3. "A Black Man, My Point of View on Improving Male and Female Relationships"

4. "Guide to Practicing the Egyptian Mysteries."

Lawrence's African Kamitic name of Anpu Waset means "Opener of the Way" and he uses the wisdom of ancient philosophies and religion as a guide to fresh insights for himself and others. He is a practitioner of Egyptian Yoga, meditation and vegetarianism along with being a father and grandfather.